KETO

COOKBOOK

Easy And Delicious High-Fat And Low-Carb Plant Based Recipes To Lose Weight Quickly. Reset And Cleanse Your Body With A Ketogenic Dict To Kickstart Λ Healthy Lifestyle

Amy J. Sullivan

Introduction

The Keto Vegan diet is a Low Carbohydrate High Fat diet that excludes all animal-based foods (e.g. meat, eggs, and dairy products). The traditional keto diet includes a lot of meat for protein, but it is not a requirement to eat meat on the keto diet. It is due that the most essential principle of the diet is fat, which you can get from vegan foods.

The ketogenic diet promotes real, single-ingredient foods as a high-quality source of vitamins, minerals, and other beneficial nutrients. You can watch your portions, exercise and think positive, but if you do not eat real foods, you can't expect a real transformation. The real food is whole, unprocessed food that is rich in nutrients and free of chemical additives. Additionally, you should cook real food at home, and you will be thankful after!

The keto vegan diet is a solution for those who want to lose weight and attain better health with the ketogenic diet…without all of the animal fats and proteins typical of the diet.

How Vegan Ketogenic Works

Both the vegan and ketogenic diets are quite different from the average American diet. However, just because they are different from what you are used to doesn't mean it has to be difficult, confusing, or unsatisfying. On the contrary, you can follow a simple step by step process to adopt the vegan ketogenic life and enjoy satisfying food to its fullest, happy to know that the same food you enjoy can also benefit your health.

Most people don't think that vegan and ketogenic diets can go hand-in-hand. When they think keto, they consider cheese, eggs, butter, and meat. Yet, combining the two into one is much easier than people first believe, all it takes is a little knowledge.

When you pair the vegan and ketogenic lifestyles together you can experience weight loss, health benefits, and satisfaction like never before. In this subtopic, you will learn how to do just that, combining the two together in the simplest method. However, feel free to adjust your diet to your own taste. Maybe you feel like you want to remove grains or meats more quickly than other people, or perhaps you feel the need to slow down and remove these non-vegan and high-carb foods more slowly. Whatever you need, listen to your body and take the lifestyle one step at a time. Remember, this is not a journey of a single day, rather one you hope to continue to make day after day. Allow yourself to take the time you need to make the change easily and healthfully, in a way that causes you little to no stress.

If you have ever been either vegan or ketogenic in the past and didn't find you lost weight, don't give up hope. When these two lifestyles are combined into one it has many more benefits, including accelerated weight maintenance. Once you begin the vegan ketogenic diet, give yourself a full two months on the diet (after removing the non-vegan and high-carb foods) before deciding how it is going for you. Some people will judge that the lifestyle is too hard or makes them too fatigued during the first month. However, if you give yourself a full two months eating a vegan ketogenic diet, we are sure you will adjust in mind and body, experiencing increased weight loss, a boost in energy, better health, and a clearer mind.

When beginning your vegan and ketogenic lifestyle you want to make changes in steps, rather than all at once. Of course, there is the occasional person who finds it easier to make all the changes overnight and adjust over time. However, for most people, it is easier and less frustrating to make changes in small steps until they gradually work up to being completely vegan and keto. Take whichever method works best for you, but don't feel as if you have to jump right in. It is better to proceed in a manner that will help you maintain the diet long-term than diving in head-first.

Chapter.1   Keto Vegan Basic Rules

As you can probably tell, there are always multiple reasons to go on a certain diet. Whatever your goals are when it's down to your overall health, there is no one diet for all. For this reason, combining the Vegan diet and the Ketogenic Diet may be excellent match for you.

By combining the two diets, you will be getting the best of both worlds! From the vegan side, you will stop animals from suffering, improve your health, and be an advocate for climate change, and from the ketogenic side, you will be able to improve health conditions such as epilepsy, Alzheimer's disease, diabetes, and obesity!

As we dive into the vegan ketogenic diet, you will find that this is going to be a more restrictive diet compared to doing either of the diets by themselves, but as long as you follow some of the basic rules, you should be able to get a grip of the concept in no time!

Rule Number One: Eliminate Meat

This rule comes from the vegan side of the diet. If you are already vegan, this step may be slightly easier for you. The very first step of your diet is going to be avoid all the meat products from your diet. These products include all eggs, dairy, fish, and meat.

Rule Number Two: Limit Carbohydrates

Now from the ketogenic side, you have the second golden rule of following a keto-vegan diet. While following this version of the diet, you will want to limit your daily carb consumption to 35g of carbohydrates. As you first begin the diet, this may be one of the most difficult parts of starting a ketogenic diet.

Rule Number Three: Vegetables

From what we said above, you may feel that vegetables are out of the diet, but it is truly a matter of finding the proper vegetables you will be able to eat. Luckily, you will still have a wide selection of low-carb vegetables to include on your new diet. Some of the more popular sources of low-carb vegetables are as follow:

- Broccoli Raab

- Watercress

- Bok Choi

- Celery

- Spinach

- Mustard Greens

- Asparagus

- Radish

- Avocado

- Arugula

- Zucchini

- Swiss Chard

- Mushrooms

- Tomato

- Olives

- Eggplant

- Bell Pepper

- Cauliflower

- Cabbage

- Bamboo Shoots

- Cucumber

- Jalapeno Pepper

- Artichoke Hearts

- Broccoli

- Bean Sprouts

- Okra

- Green Beans

- Snow Peas

- Turnips

And more!

Rule Number Four: Plant-Based Fats

By following a keto-vegan diet, you will want to make sure that 70% of your calories in a day are coming from plant-based fats. As you probably already well know, there are good and bad fats. No, you can't just sit down and eat a container of butter. Instead, you will want to look for middle chain triglycerides to help fuel your body.

As far as fats go, you will want to avoid any trans or saturated fats. These are the fats that cause disease, cholesterol problems, and heart issues.

Luckily, many of these fats are found in packaged foods, meat, and dairy, all of which you will be avoiding while following your new, keto-vegan diet! Instead, you will want to look for foods, including:

Seeds

Seeds are a great source of fat to include in your new diet, especially because they can be used in many recipes. Seeds are typically high in omega-3s, which will be important as you begin to balance your diet.

Nuts

Another food source you will be using for fat will be nuts. While these are also a great source for protein, they also contain a good amount of monounsaturated fats that can help reduce your risk for heart disease.

Coconut Oil

The third source of fat for the keto-vegan diet is going to be coconut oil. The good factor of coconut oil is that you can use it for cooking while giving your food a nice hint of flavor. Coconut oil also has a number of benefits by itself, including weight loss, bone growth, improvements to heart health, and may also be able to ease your digestion!

Along with coconut oil, there is a number of different oils you can add to your diet to help incorporate more fat sources. These oils include Olive Oil, Avocado Oil, Red Palm Oil, and MCT Oil.

Avocado

On the keto-vegan diet, avocado is about to become your best friend! The popularity of avocados has been on the rise for a good reason! The best part is that avocados are very versatile to keep your diet new and exciting from week to week. Whether you enjoy your avocado whole or as guacamole, it is welcome on your new diet. Avocados are packed with monounsaturated fat and will be an excellent source for you to include.

Cacao Nibs

Yes, you read that correctly! Chocolate will be included in your diet, as long as it is done correctly. Unfortunately, some of your favorite candy bars are most likely not made from cacao nibs. Instead, you will want to search for dark chocolate! Dark chocolate will provide you with antioxidants and good levels of monounsaturated fats. Being that you are on a vegan-ketogenic diet, make sure that the chocolate is vegan-friendly.

Rule Number Five: Plant-based Protein

There is a common misconception that vegans will never be able to get the proper amount of proteins if they are not eating meat. The truth is, there are plenty of sources you will be able to enjoy while sticking to the rules of your diet. As far as the keto-vegan diet goes, you will want 25% of your calories to come from a protein that is plant-based.

Tofu & Tempeh

When it comes to soy products, you will find that these will generally be the richest source of protein for you. In a one-half cup of firm tofu, you will be getting about 10g of protein. If tempeh is more your style, you can get 15g of protein for just half of a cup!

Tofu will be a staple in your diet because it is incredibly versatile. As you learn to cook tofu the proper way, you will find that the protein takes on the flavor on any recipes you put it in! It can also be enjoyed as a substitute for soups, sandwiches, and basically any meat dish you think you are going to miss on the ketogenic diet.

Peanuts & Almonds

Peanuts and almonds will be an excellent source of protein because they can be enjoyed as part of a meal or as a quick snack. Peanuts are full of healthy fats and will provide you with 20.5g of protein per ½ cup, and almonds can give you 16.5g of protein per ½ cup. The almonds are also beneficial for skin and eyes due to the fact that they contain a good amount of vitamin E.

Spirulina

Spiru-what? If you have never heard of this source of protein, you are not alone! As you begin such a strict diet, you will need to start getting creative when it comes to your food sources! Spirulina is a green or blue algae. Typically, two tablespoons will give you a whopping 8g of protein! It also has other wonderful nutrients, including manganese, iron, and B vitamins.

Chia & Hemp Seeds

Seeds are always an excellent item to have in your cabinets because they will be great sources for fat and protein. On top of these benefits, seeds are generally low in calories as well, meaning more weight loss! Chia seeds will provide you with 2g of protein per tablespoon and are considered a complete source of protein.

Hemp seeds offer a whopping 5g of protein per tablespoon! Just like with the chia seeds, they are a complete source of protein and can be used easily in a number of different dishes.

Leafy Green Vegetables

The next popular source of protein comes from dark-colored and leafy green vegetables. For example, one stalk of protein will contain 2g of protein, and one cup of kale offers 2g of protein. While this isn't enough by themselves, you can add them to other dishes, including tofu, nuts, and seeds, to really help pack a punch.

Rule Number Six: Know Your Replacements

As you begin following this diet on your own, just know that with many of the recipes you find, there is always a replacement for cheese, eggs, and milk! In the modern market, there are plenty of keto-friendly dairy and egg replacements for you to enjoy. Here are the popular alternatives to use.

- Regular milk replaced with Coconut Milk

- Heavy cream replaced with Coconut Cream

- Butter replaced by Vegan Butter or Coconut Oil

- Cheese replaced by Vegan Cheese

- Cream Cheese replaced by Vegan Soft Cheese

- Yogurt and Sour Cream replaced by Nut-based Yogurt

Egg Substitutes

Egg substitutes are key to success while following the keto-vegan diet. There are going to be many almost-vegan recipes that you will want to try, but eggs will be standing in your way.

Flaxseed is one of the best substitutes to date. Luckily, the nutty flavor from the flax seed works well with baked goods. All you will need to do is mix one tablespoon of flaxseed with three tablespoons of water to make one "egg."

Another great alternative is silken tofu. This is a softer form of tofu that can be pureed when you need to replace an egg within a recipe. It will take ¼ of a cup of this to replace 1 egg.

Rule Number Seven: Find Your Macros

On the Ketogenic Diet, it will be vital that you find your specific macros for your diet. Being that we all have different goals, different bodies, and different lifestyles, there is no one correct way to follow a keto-vegan diet. Instead, you will want to use an online keto calculator to help you find the proper amounts of protein, carbs, and fats you will need to reach your goals.

As you can clearly see, it is easier than expected if you do wish to follow both the ketogenic diet and the vegan lifestyle. With so many alternatives on the market, you will be able to make just about any recipe you want vegan-friendly.

Chapter. 2.   Keto Vegan

1. Asian Chickpea Pancake

Prep time: 5 minutes

Cooking time: 10 minutes

Serves: 1

Ingredients:

- 34 g green onion, chopped
- 34 g red pepper, thinly sliced
- 70 g chickpea powder
- 1 1/2 g garlic powder
- 1 1/4 g baking powder
- 1 1/2 g salt
- ¼ g, chili flakes

Directions:

1. Mix all the fixings in a bowl until you see air bubbles. Add the chopped veggies and after one final stir, add the mixture to a preheated skillet, and allow it to spread evenly over the pan for about 5 minutes.
2. Once the underside is cooked through, flip and let it cook for an additional 5 minutes, and once you are done, simply plate and serve.

Nutrition:

Calories 227

Carbohydrates 38 g

Fats 3.6 g

Protein 12 g

2. Overnight Oat Bowl

Prep time: 10 minutes

Cooking time: 10 minutes

Serves: 2

Ingredients:

- 15 g chia seeds
- 75 g hemp hearts
- 14 g sweetener
- 2/3 cup coconut milk
- ¼ g vanilla extract/vanilla bean

- 1 1/4 grams of salt

Directions:

1. Mix in all of your fixings and allow the bowl to sit overnight in a covered container to avoid evaporation. Serve.

Nutrition:

Calories 634

Carbohydrates 17 g

Fats 52.32 g

Protein 27.75 g

3. Coconut Crepes

Prep time: 10 minutes

Cooking time: 8 minutes

Serves: 3

Ingredients:

- 15 g virgin coconut oil
- ¼ cup almond milk
- ¼ cup coconut milk
- ¼ g vanilla essence
- 30 g coconut flour
- 15 g almond meal
- 1 cup applesauce

Directions:

1. Dump all of your fixings into one large bowl and whisk until smooth. Set aside within 10 minutes.
2. In the meantime, lightly oil a frying pan on the stove, and pour in the batter and spread until the pan is coated with a thin layer.
3. Cook for a couple minutes until the crepe starts to get crispy, and flip. Another minute on the stove and you are ready to serve, alongside your toppings of choice or course.

Nutrition:

Calories 137

Carbohydrates 12.15 g

Fats 16.54 g

Protein 1 g

4. Low-Carb Breakfast "Couscous"

Prep time: 10 minutes

Cooking time: 2 minutes

Serves: 4

Ingredients:

- 200 g cauliflower, riced
- 30 g strawberries
- 20 g almonds
- 20 g flax seeds
- 60 g mandarin segments
- 1 cup coconut milk
- 1 tbsp erythritol

- ¼ tsp cinnamon powder
- 3 tbsp rose water

Directions:

1. Mix all fixings in a microwave safe bowl. Cook for 2 minutes at 30-second intervals. Serve.

Nutrition:

Calories 190

Carbohydrates 9 g

Fats 17 g

Protein 3 g

5. Gingerbread-Spiced Breakfast Smoothie

Prep time: 2 minutes

Cooking time: 0 minutes

Serves: 2

Ingredients:

- 1 cup coconut milk
- 1 bag tea
- ¼ tsp cinnamon powder
- 1/8 tsp nutmeg powder
- 1/8 tsp powdered cloves
- 1/3 cup chia seeds
- 2 tbsp flax seeds

Directions:

1. Put the teabag in your mug then pour in a cup of hot water. Allow to steep for a few minutes.
2. Pour the tea into a blender together with the rest of the ingredients. Process until smooth.

Nutrition:

Calories 449

Carbohydrates 10 g

Fats 46 g

Protein 6 g

6. Vegan Breakfast Muffins

Prep time: 5 minutes

Cooking time: 3 minutes

Serves: 3

Ingredients:

- 2 tbsp almond flour
- ½ tsp baking powder
- ½ tsp salt
- 2 tbsp ground flax seeds

- ¼ cup coconut milk
- 3 tbsp avocado oil

Directions:

1. Whisk the almond flour, ground flax, baking powder, and salt in a bowl. Stir in coconut milk.
2. Heat avocado oil in a non-stick pan. Ladle in the batter then cook within 2 to 3 minutes each side. Serve.

Nutrition:

Calories 194

Carbohydrates 2 g

Fats 21 g

Protein 1 g

7. Vegan Breakfast Biscuits

Prep time: 10 minutes

Cooking time: 10 minutes

Serves: 6

Ingredients:

- 1 1/2 cups almond flour
- 1 tbsp baking powder
- ¼ tsp salt
- ½ tsp onion powder
- ½ cup coconut milk
- ¼ cup nutritional yeast
- 2 tbsp ground flax seeds
- ¼ cup olive oil

Directions:

1. Warm your oven to 450°F. Whisk all the fixings in a bowl. Divide the batter into your oiled muffin tin. Bake within 10 minutes. Serve.

Nutrition:

Calories 306

Carbohydrates 10 g

Fats 28 g

Protein 7 g

8. Avocado Mug Bread

Prep time: 2 minutes

Cooking time: 2 minutes

Serves: 1

Ingredients:

- ¼ cup Almond Flour
- ½ tsp Baking Powder
- ¼ tsp Salt
- ¼ cup Mashed Avocados
- 1 tbsp Coconut Oil

Directions:

1. Mix all the fixings in a microwave-safe mug. Microwave within 90 seconds. Cool within 2 minutes. Serve.

Nutrition:

Calories 317

Carbohydrates 9 g

Fats 30 g

Protein 6 g

9. Vegan Breakfast Sausages

Prep time: 15 minutes

Cooking time: 12 minutes

Serves: 4

Ingredients:

- 200 g portobella mushrooms
- 150 g walnuts
- 1 tbsp tomato paste
- 75 g panko
- 1 tsp paprika
- 1 tsp dried sage
- 1 tsp salt

- ½ tsp black pepper

Directions:

1. Blend all the fixings in a food processor. Divide mixture into serving-sized portions and shape into sausages. Bake for 12 minutes at 375°F. Serve.

Nutrition:

Calories 271

Carbohydrates 9 g

Fats 25 g

Protein 7 g

10. Quick Breakfast Yogurt

Prep time: 2 minutes

Cooking time: 8 minutes

Serves: 6

Ingredients:

- 4 cups full-fat coconut milk
- 2 tbsp coconut milk powder
- 100 g strawberries, for serving

Directions:

1. Whisk the coconut milk and milk powder in a microwave safe bowl. Heat on high for 8-9 minutes. Top with fresh strawberries and choice of sweetener to serve.

Nutrition:

Calories 186

Carbohydrates 10 g

Fats 38 g

Protein 4 g

11. Spiced Tofu and Broccoli Scramble

Prep time: 5 minutes

Cooking time: 3 minutes

Serves: 3

Ingredients:

- 400 g firm tofu, drained and pressed
- 1 tbsp tamari
- 1 tbsp garlic powder
- 2 tsp paprika powder
- 2 tsp turmeric powder
- 150 g broccoli, rough-chopped
- 2 tbsp olive oil

Directions:

1. Crumble the tofu in a bowl with the garlic powder, paprika, turmeric, and nutritional yeast. Heat olive oil in a pan.
2. Sautee broccoli for a minute. Stir in spiced tofu. Cook for 1-2 minutes. Season with tamari. Serve hot.

Nutrition:

Calories 231

Carbohydrates 7 g

Fats 17 g

Protein 16 g

12. Meat-Free Breakfast Chili

Prep time: 10 minutes

Cooking time: 20 minutes

Serves: 4

Ingredients:

- 400 g textured-vegetable protein
- ¼ cup red kidney beans
- ½ cup canned diced tomatoes
- 1 large bell pepper, diced
- 1 large white onion, diced
- 1 tsp cumin powder
- 1 tsp chili powder
- 1 tsp paprika
- 1 tsp garlic powder
- ½ tsp dried oregano
- 2 cups Water

Directions:

1. Combine all the fixings in a pot. Simmer for 20 minutes. Serve with your favorite bread or some slices of fresh avocado.

Nutrition:

Calories 174

Carbohydrates 9 g

Fats 9 g

Protein 18 g

13. Vegan Southwestern Breakfast

Prep time: 10 minutes

Cooking time: 5 minutes

Serves: 6

Ingredients:

- 1 small white onion, diced
- 1 bell pepper, diced
- 150 g mushrooms, sliced
- 400 grams firm tofu, crumbled
- 1 tsp turmeric powder
- 1 tbsp garlic powder
- 2 tbsp nutritional yeast
- ¼ cup chopped green onions
- 2 cups fresh spinach
- 1 cup cherry tomatoes
- 2 cups baked beans
- 2 tbsp olive oil

Directions:

1. Sautee onions, bell peppers, and mushrooms until onions are translucent. Add in the tofu. Stir in the turmeric, garlic powder, and nutritional yeast.
2. Add green onions and spinach. Sautee for 1-2 minutes. Serve with baked beans and cherry tomatoes.

Nutrition:

Calories 174

Carbohydrates 10 g

Fats 10 g

Protein 13 g

14. Tofu Seitan

Prep time: 10 minutes

Cooking time: 12 minutes

Serves: 6

Ingredients:

- ½ tsp salt
- 1 tsp garlic, powdered
- 2 tsp vegetable broth
- 1 tbsp onion, powdered
- 2 tbsp nutritional yeast
- 2 tbsp water
- 1 ¼ cup tofu
- 1 ½ cup vital wheat gluten

Directions:

1. Stir the fixings in a bowl until a dough forms. Dust your countertop plus your hands using wheat gluten.
2. Form a ball shape out of your dough; do not knead. Slice it into 6 pieces. Press each of your ball into an oval shape, 4x6". Put the inside your pot, fill with water then let it boil.
3. Put the seitan in it; steam within 12 minutes, flipping it to cook both sides. Remove then let it cool within 1 hour, or so. Serve.

Nutrition:

Calories: 160

Carbohydrates: 7 g

Proteins: 30 g

Fats: 3 g

15. Chimichurri Roasted Butternut Squash

Prep time: 10 minutes

Cooking time: 15 minutes

Serves: 3

Ingredients:

- ½ cup of quinoa
- 2 cups of mushrooms, sliced
- ¼ cup of goji berries
- 1 acorn squash, cut into 4-6 moon-shaped slices
- 2 tablespoon olive oil (best if extra virgin)
- 1 tablespoon coconut oil
- 1 cup of water
- 1 cup onion, thinly diced
- 2 cloves garlic

Chimichurri Sauce:

- 1 cup of parsley
- 2 tablespoon lime
- ½ cup of olive oil, extra virgin
- 1 tablespoon sherry vinegar
- 3 cloves garlic
- 1 shallot
- ¼ teaspoon cayenne pepper
- ½ teaspoon salt

Directions:

1. Warm your broiler. For the chimichurri sauce, mix the parsley, garlic, shallot, vinegar, cayenne pepper, lime juice, plus ½ cup of olive oil in a bowl.
2. Set an aluminum-foiled cookie sheet. Place the acorn squash slices in it then put some olive oil on top. Charred to your desired liking.
3. Let a medium saucepan filled with water boil then simmer the quinoa within 10 minutes. Warm-up a skillet on medium heat, then cook the onions in it.
4. Put in the mushroom plus garlic, cook on low within 5 minutes. Serve the squash with quinoa plus mushroom on top. Put the goji berries then the chimichurri sauce. Serve!

Nutrition:

Calories: 615

Proteins: 12.5 g

Carbohydrates: 71.6 g

Fats: 35.7 g

16. Eggplant Pizza

Prep time: 10 minutes

Cooking time: 35 minutes

Serves: 8

Ingredients:

- 2 tablespoon olive oil
- ¼ teaspoon pepper
- ¼ teaspoon salt
- ½ teaspoon oregano, dried
- 1 cup of panko
- ½ tablespoon almond flour
- 1 tablespoon flaxseed, ground

- 1/3 cup of water
- ½ eggplant, medium, sliced into ¼-inch triangles
- 2 cup of marinara sauce
- 1 lb. vegan pizza dough

For the cheese:

- 2 tablespoon almond milk, unsweetened
- ½ cup of cashews, soaked in water within 6 hours & drained
- 3 tablespoon lemon juice, squeezed
- ¼ lb. tofu, extra firm drained

Directions:

1. Warm your oven at 400 F; coat a cookie sheet using ½ tbsp of olive oil. Whisk the flaxseed, flour, plus water in a bowl.
2. Mix the salt, pepper, oregano, plus panko in a separate bowl. Soak each eggplant slices into your flaxseed batter then with panko batter and put it on your cookie sheet.
3. Bake within 15 minutes. Flip then bake again within 15 minutes. Remove and set aside.
4. Flour your clean workspace, then work the dough to a 14" circle using a rolling pin, work then transfer it in your pizza pan. Oiled the dough using olive oil then bake within 20 minutes.
5. For the cheese, blend the cashews in your blender until crumbly. Put the lemon juice, almond milk, plus tofu; then blend it again until chunky. Set aside.
6. Put marinara sauce to your cooked crust, put the eggplant slices, then the cheese on top. Serve!

Nutrition:

Calories: 234

Carbohydrates: 27 g

Proteins: 5.4 g

Fats: 12 g

17. Avocado Carbonara

Prep time: 10 minutes

Cooking time: 20 minutes

Serves: 1

Ingredients:

- Parsley, as needed
- Spinach angel hair pasta, cooked
- 2 tsp EVOO
- 2 cloves garlic, minced
- ½ lemon, juice &zest
- 1 avocado flesh
- Salt, as needed
- Pepper, as needed

Directions:

1. For the sauce, blend the parsley, olive oil, garlic, lemon, plus avocado using a food processor.
2. Put the noodles in your bowl, then put the blended sauce on top. Flavor it with pepper plus salt, and serve!

Nutrition:

Calories: 526

Carbohydrates: 24.6 g

Proteins: 5.8 g

Fats: 48.7 g

18. Curried Tofu

Prep time: 5 minutes

Cooking time: 30 minutes

Serves: 4

Ingredients:

- ¼ tsp garlic powder
- 2 tbsp curry powder
- 1 pack extra firm tofu, cubes

Directions:

1. Heat to 400 F the oven. Put the garlic powder, curry powder, plus tofu in your container with lid. Shake to coat.
2. Put on your cookie sheet with parchment paper, then bake within 15 minutes, flip then bake again within 15 minutes. Serve!

Nutrition:

Calories: 333

Carbohydrates: 35 g

Proteins: 34 g

Fats: 7 g

19. Sesame Tofu and Eggplant

Prep time: 15 minutes

Cooking time: 30 minutes

Serves: 4

Ingredients:

- 1 pound firm tofu, blotted to remove excess moisture, slice into 8
- 1 cup cilantro, diced
- 1 eggplant
- 1 tsp red pepper flakes, crushed
- ¼ cup sesame seeds
- 4 tbsp sesame oil, toasted
- ¼ cup soy sauce
- 3 tbsp rice vinegar
- 1 tbsp olive oil
- 2 tsp sweetener
- 2 cloves garlic
- Salt, as needed
- Pepper, as needed

Directions:

1. Set the oven to 200 F. For the marinade, mix the red pepper flakes, garlic, sesame oil, vinegar, plus ¼ cup of cilantro in a mixing bowl.
2. Julienne your eggplant using a mandolin. Mix the noodles plus the marinade in your bowl.
3. Warm-up oil to your skillet on medium-low heat, then cook your eggplant. Turn off your oven, then put the rest of your cilantro.

4. Move the eggplants in your oven-safe dish, wrap it using foil, then put in the oven. Coat your tofu using sesame seeds.
5. Warm-up 2 tbsp of sesame oil in your skillet on medium heat. Fry the tofu within 5 minutes flipping it occasionally.
6. Coat the tofu with the soy sauce into your pan, until it caramelized. Remove your noodles from the oven then put the caramelized tofu on top. Serve!

Nutrition:

Calories: 295

Proteins: 11.21 g

Carbohydrates: 6.87 g

Fats: 6.87 g

20. Tempeh Coconut Curry

Prep time: 10 minutes

Cooking time: 23 minutes

Serves: 4

Ingredients:

Curry:

- 2 tsp low-sodium soy sauce
- 2 tsp tamarind pulp
- 1 tbsp lime juice
- 1 tbsp garlic, finely chopped
- 1 tbsp ginger, finely chopped
- 1 tbsp vegetable oil
- Salt, as needed
- 8 oz. tempeh
- 13 1/2 oz. coconut milk, light
- 1 cup water
- 3 cups sweet potato, chopped
- 1 cinnamon stick
- ½ tsp red pepper, crushed
- ½ tsp turmeric, ground
- 1 ½ tsp coriander, ground
- 2 cups onion, diced

Rice:

- 1 ½ cup of cauliflower rice, cooked
- 1/3 cup of cilantro, chopped
- ¼ tsp salt

Directions:

1. Warm-up some oil in your nonstick pot on medium-high heat. Put the onion plus ½ tsp salt, sautéing within 2 minutes.
2. Mix in the tamarind, crumbling it in your skillet then cook within 2 minutes. Put in the coriander, ginger, red pepper, turmeric, garlic, plus cinnamon stick, and mix.
3. Put in more salt, tempeh, milk, water, plus potatoes, and let it boil. Simmer within 15 minutes.
4. Mix in the soy sauce then simmer it again within 3 minutes. Discard the cinnamon stick. Mix in the cilantro plus the cooked cauliflower rice. Put in it in a bowl then the curry. Serve!

Nutrition:

Calories: 558

Proteins: 18.4 g

Carbohydrates: 54.2 g

Fats: 33.5 g

21. Tempeh Tikka Masala

Prep time: 10 minutes

Cooking time: 20 minutes

Serves: 3

Ingredients:

Tempeh:

- 8 oz. tempeh, cubed
- ½ tsp sea salt
- 1 tsp gram masala
- 1 tsp ginger, ground
- 1 tsp cumin, ground
- 2 tsp apple cider vinegar
- ½ cup of vegan yogurt

Tikka Masala Sauce:

- 1 cup of coconut milk, full-fat
- 1 cup of tomato sauce
- 2 cups frozen peas
- ¼ tsp turmeric
- 1 tsp chili powder
- 1 tsp garam masala
- 1/4 cup of ginger, freshly grated
- 3 cloves garlic, minced
- 1 onion, diced
- 1 tbsp coconut oil
- ½ tsp sea salt

Directions:

1. For the tempeh, mix the ginger, garam masala, vinegar, sea salt, cumin, plus yogurt in your bowl. Put the tempeh then mix it well; wrap your bowl then chill within 60 minutes.
2. Warm-up some coconut oil on medium heat in a pan. Cook in the garlic, ginger, plus onion within 5 minutes. Put the garam masala, sea salt, chili powder, plus turmeric then mix it well.
3. Put the frozen peas, tomato sauce, coconut, milk, plus tempeh, adjust your heat to medium. Simmer within 15 minutes. Serve.

Nutrition:

Calories: 422

Carbohydrates: 29 g

Proteins: 22 g

Fats: 24 g

22. Cheesy Brussel Sprout Bake

Prep time: 15 minutes

Cooking time: 46 minutes

Serves: 8

Ingredients:

- ½ onion sliced
- 2 tbsp garlic, chopped
- 2 tbsp avocado oil
- 1 ½ lb. Brussel sprouts, trimmed

Cheese:

- Dash cayenne, as needed
- 1 tsp onion powder
- 1 tsp salt
- ¼ tsp pepper
- ¼ tsp paprika
- ½ tsp garlic, powder
- ½ tsp thyme
- 1 tbsp tapioca starch
- ¼ cup nutritional yeast
- ½ cup vegetable broth
- 1 can coconut cream

Crumble Topping:

- ¼ tsp pepper
- ½ tsp garlic, powder
- 1 tsp salt
- ½ cup panko crumbs

Directions:

1. Warm the oven to 425 F. Steam the Brussel sprouts within 10 minutes. Oiled your baking dish using nonstick spray. Put the Brussel sprouts then set side.
2. Set your skillet to medium heat then mix in the garlic, avocado oil, plus onion, cook within 6 minutes. Put this on your Brussel sprouts.
3. Cook the vegetable broth, nutritional yeast, coconut cream, garlic, paprika, onion powder, thyme, salt, plus pepper, whisking to combine, in the same skillet on low heat.
4. Put in the tapioca starch then mix occasionally within 5 minutes to thicken until it form to a cheese-like sauce mixture. Put this on the Brussel sprouts and onions.
5. Mix the panko, salt, garlic, plus pepper in a mixing container until crumble. Put it over the cheese mixture. Bake within 25 minutes, then serve.

Nutrition:

Calories: 116

Proteins: 4 g

Carbohydrates: 16 g

Fats: 4 g

23. Tofu Noodles

Prep time: 10 minutes

Cooking time: 20 minutes

Serves: 4

Ingredients:

- 1 tbsp lime juice
- 6 oz. Thai rice noodles, cooked
- 1 red bell pepper, chopped
- ¼ cup cilantro, minced
- ¼ cup peanuts, diced
- 2 packs baked tofu
- ½ tsp black pepper, ground
- 2 tsp turmeric, ground
- 1 tbsp ginger, minced
- 2 cup vegetable stock
- 4 heads baby bok choy, diced
- 2 carrots, julienned
- 2 cloves garlic, diced
- ½ red onion, diced
- 1 tsp peanut oil
- 2 tsp garlic chili sauce

Directions:

1. Warm-up the peanut oil in a pan on medium-high heat. Cook the ginger, garlic, plus onion within 5 minutes. Put in the carrots plus bell pepper, mixing occasionally then cook within 5 minutes.
2. Mix the turmeric, lime juice, chili sauce, black pepper, plus vegetable stock, and mix in the pan of peppers plus carrots.

3. Let it boil, then adjust to low heat, and cook within 5 minutes. Put the noodles, bok choy, plus tofu then cook again within 5 minutes. Serve with the chili peppers, peanuts, plus cilantro.

Nutrition:

Calories: 669

Proteins: 55.1g

Carbohydrates: 69g

Fats: 25g

24. Cashew Siam Salad

Prep time: 10 minutes

Cooking time: 15 minutes

Serves: 3

Ingredients:

- 1 teaspoon olive oil
- 1 cup of cashews, chopped
- 3 green onions, diced
- 1 bag slaw mix
- 2/3 cup of sunflower seeds
- 2 packs ramen noodles

Dressing:

- 1 cup of vinegar
- ½ cup of sweetener
- ramen noodles seasonings

Directions:

1. Warm your oven at 350 F. Mix the cashews plus oil in a mixing bowl. Put the nuts on your cookie sheet then toast.
2. Mix the crumbled ramen noodles, slaw mix, sunflower seeds, plus green onion in a separate mixing bowl.
3. Mix the vinegar plus sweetener in a small bowl. Remove the peanuts in your oven then let it cool. Put the salad in your bowl then put the cashews on top. Put the dressing and serve.

Nutrition:

Calories: 352

Carbohydrates: 26.6 g

Proteins: 9.6 g

Fats: 24.5 g

25. Edamame Cucumber Salad

Prep time: 10 minutes

Cooking time: 0 minutes

Serves: 6

Ingredients:

- 4 English cucumbers, spiralized into noodles, discard excess moisture
- 1 jalapeno pepper, diced
- 2 cups frozen edamame, shelled & thawed

Vinaigrette:

- 1 tsp red pepper flakes
- 1 ½ tsp garlic
- 1 ½ tsp Dijon mustard
- 1 ½ tsp soy sauce, low-sodium
- 2 tsp ginger, paste
- 3 tsp toasted sesame oil
- 1/3 cup rice vinegar
- 1/3 cup EVOO

Directions:

1. Mix the cucumber noodles, jalapeno, red bell pepper, plus edamame in a mixing bowl, and set aside.
2. For the vinaigrette, mix the garlic, red pepper flakes ginger, Dijon mustard, soy sauce, oil, rice vinegar, plus olive oil in a separate mixing container.
3. Mix the salad plus dressing, wrap then let it chill within 2 hours or overnight. Serve.

Nutrition:

Calories: 166

Proteins: 2.9 g

Carbohydrates: 6.4 g

Fats: 14.9 g

26. Mushroom Lettuce Wraps

Prep time: 5 minutes

Cooking time: 6 minutes

Serves: 3-5

Ingredients:

- 8 oz. mushrooms, diced
- 1 can water chestnuts
- 12 oz. tofu, extra firm, remove excess moisture
- 8 leaves of romaine lettuce
- 4 green onions, minced
- ¼ tsp red pepper flakes
- 2 tsp ginger, diced
- 2 tsp canola oil
- 2 cloves garlic, diced

- 1 tsp sesame oil
- 2 tablespoon rice vinegar
- 3 tablespoon soy sauce, reduced-sodium
- 3 tablespoon hoisin Sauce

Directions:

1. Mix the sesame oil, soy sauce, rice vinegar, plus hoisin in a bowl, and set aside. Warm-up the 2 tsp of canola oil in a big skillet on medium-high heat.
2. Break the tofu into small pieces then cook within 5 minutes. Put in the mushrooms then cook until the liquid almost evaporates.
3. Put in the red pepper, garlic, green onions, ginger, plus chestnuts then cook within 30 seconds. Put the sauce into your skillet then cook until warmed. Put the tofu mixture into lettuce wraps and serve.

Nutrition:

Calories: 265

Carbohydrates: 37.6g

Proteins: 13.6 g

Fats: 7.9 g

27. Asparagus and Mushrooms with Cauliflower Risotto

Prep time: 5 minutes

Cooking time: 13 minutes

Serves: 2

Ingredients:

- ½ onion, large, diced
- 7 ½ oz cauliflower rice
- 1 garlic clove, diced
- 2 tbsp olive oil
- 3 oz asparagus, trimmed into ½-inch
- 4 oz mushrooms, slice
- 1 tbsp lemon juice
- 3 tbsp white wine
- ½ zest of lemon zest
- 2 tbsp parsley, finely chopped

Directions:

1. Cook the garlic plus onions in your warmed skillet with some oil within 3 to 5 minutes. Toss in the mushrooms and continue cooking slowly for another minute.
2. Mix in the asparagus then cook within 2 to 3 minutes. Pour in the wine, lemon juice, and cauliflower rice. Cook until tender for approximately 5-10 minutes. Season to your liking and serve.

Nutrition:

Calories: 268

Carbs: 13g

Fat: 5g

Protein: 47g

28. Asparagus and Tofu Stir Fry

Prep time: 10 minutes

Cooking time: 4 minutes

Serves: 3

Ingredients:

- 8 oz sliced extra-firm tofu
- 1 tbsp ginger, peeled and grated
- 1 to 2 spritz sesame oil
- 4 thinly sliced green onions
- 1 handful toasted and chopped cashew nuts
- 1 bunch tripped and chopped asparagus
- 2 tbsp hoisin sauce
- 1 handful basil
- 1 handful mint
- 1 lime, zest and juice
- 3 handful chopped spinach
- 1 pinch salt
- 3 garlic cloves, chopped

Directions:

1. Prepare a wok with the oil and cook the tofu for a few minutes. Place on a platter. Warm more oil and sauté the pepper flakes with the asparagus, onions, salt, and grated ginger. Cook for 1 minute.
2. Toss in the cashews, garlic, and spinach. Continue cooking for 1-2 minutes. Add the tofu back in the mixture and add the lime juice, zest, and hoisin sauce.

3. Continue stir-frying for another 20 seconds. Serve with the mint plus basil.

Nutrition:

Calories: 250

Carbs: 5g

Fat: 13g

Protein: 27g

29. Broccoli Noodles and Tofu

Prep time: 5 minutes

Cooking time: 11 minutes

Serves: 3

Ingredients:

- 2 broccoli stems, spiralized
- 2 tbsp EVOO
- ½ onion, diced
- 1 block extra-firm tofu
- 2 cloves of garlic, minced
- 1 finely diced red bell pepper
- 1 tsp cumin
- 1 tsp turmeric
- pepper and salt, as needed

Directions:

1. After a pot of water starts boiling, add the broccoli. Cook until done or about 2-3 minutes. Warm up a pan with the oil.
2. Sauté the onions, peppers, plus garlic within 3 to 4 minutes. Mix in the cumin then cook within 1 minute.
3. Mix in the rest of the fixings and cook for 2 to 3 minutes. Divide into three servings and enjoy.

Nutrition:

Calories: 242

Carbs: 5g

Fat: 15g

Protein: 23g

30. Cauliflower Tabbouleh

Prep time: 10 minutes

Cooking time: 0 minutes

Serves: 8

Ingredients:

- 2 cups lightly steamed cauliflower rice
- 1 cup fresh mint
- 1 cup fresh parsley
- 1 English cucumber
- 1 red bell pepper
- ½ lb. cherry tomatoes
- 1 red onion
- ¼ cup EVOO
- pepper and salt to taste
- ¼ cup lemon juice

Directions:

1. Toss all the fixings into a bowl. Serve and enjoy anytime.

Nutrition:

Calories: 70

Carbs: 6g

Fat: 5g

Protein: 1g

31. Collard Green Wraps

Prep time: 5 minutes

Cooking time: 0 minutes

Serves: 1

Ingredients:

- ¼ cup sliced carrots
- 2 deveined collard greens
- 2 tbsp sauerkraut
- 2 tbsp tahini sauce

Directions:

1. Combine the sauerkraut and carrots and place inside the collard leaves. Roll it into a wrap and drizzle with the sauce. Serve.

Nutrition:

Calories: 473

Carbs: 51g

Fat: 31g

Protein: 12g

32. Eggplant Lasagna

Prep time: 20 minutes

Cooking time: 45 minutes

Serves: 4

Ingredients:

- 1 sliced eggplant
- 1 cup marinara sauce
- 1 tbsp salt
- ½ cup vegan cheese of choice
- 1 cup vegan cashew ricotta
- olive oil, as needed

Directions:

1. Shake the salt over the eggplant rounds and set to the side for an hour. Rinse and pat them dry.
2. Lightly spritz a baking dish with the oil and layer the sliced eggplant on the bottom. Put the sauce then the cheese.
3. Add another layer of eggplant, ricotta, and lastly, the marinara sauce. Make one more layer of the eggplant, sauce, and cheese.
4. Bake with a lid on for 1/2 hour. Remove the cover then cook again within 15 minutes. Serve.

Nutrition:

Calories: 250

Carbs: 16g

Fat: 15g

Protein: 13g

33. Falafel with Tahini Sauce

Prep time: 10 minutes

Cooking time: 8 minutes

Serves: 2

Ingredients:

- 1 cup raw pureed cauliflower
- ½ tbsp ground coriander
- 1 tbsp ground cumin
- ½ cup ground slivered almonds
- 1 tsp kosher salt
- 1 minced garlic clove
- ½ tsp cayenne pepper
- 1 large eggs
- 2 tbsp freshly chopped parsley
- 3 tbsp coconut flour
- Ingredients for the Tahini Sauce:
- 4 tbsp water
- 2 tbsp tahini paste
- 1 tsp salt
- 1 minced garlic clove
- 1 tbsp lemon juice
- olive or grapeseed oil

Directions:

1. Use a food processor and puree enough cauliflower to make one cup with a grainy texture. Process the almonds the same way, but don't over grind.

2. Combine the fixings in a mixing bowl and add the remainder of the components of the recipe until well blended.
3. Warm up a half mixture of olive and grape seed oil. Make (eight) three-inch patties and add to the pan.
4. Cook until browned and turn them over. Four minutes for each side should be sufficient. Add them to a platter to drain on some paper towels.
5. Mix all of the tahini fixings in a bowl, adding small portions of water a little at a time until it reaches the desired thickness. Use the tahini sauce as a garnish with the tomato and parsley.

Nutrition:

Calories: 340

Carbs: 32g

Fat: 17g

Protein: 13g

34. Spinach Panini

Prep time: 10 minutes

Cooking time: 20 minutes

Serves: 1

Ingredients:

- 1 cup baby spinach
- 2 low-carb bread slices
- 4 tbsp pesto
- ½ sliced avocado
- 1 tbsp vegan butter
- pepper and salt, to your liking
- 1-2 spritz hot sauce

Directions:

1. Use a knife to spread butter onto each slice of bread (only on one side). Spread pesto on the other side.
2. Add one slice in a skillet (low heat). Add some salt and pepper. Top it off with the avocado and spinach.
3. Add the slice of bread with the butter side facing out. Prepare until golden brown within 3 to 4 minutes. Flip and do the same. Drizzle with the hot sauce and enjoy right away!

Nutrition:

Calories: 380

Carbs: 40g

Fat: 18g

Protein: 16g

35. Smoked Tempeh with Broccoli Fritters

Prep time: 15 minutes

Cooking time: 25 minutes

Serves: 4

Ingredients:

Flax egg:

- 4 tbsp flax seed powder + 12 tbsp water

Grilled tempeh:

- 1 tbsp soy sauce
- 3 tbsp olive oil
- 1 tbsp grated ginger
- 3 tbsp fresh lime juice
- Salt and cayenne pepper to taste
- 10 oz. tempeh slices

Broccoli fritters:

- 1 medium head Broccoli
- 8 oz. tofu halloumi cheese
- 3 tbsp almond flour
- ½ tsp onion powder
- 1 tsp salt
- ¼ tsp freshly ground black pepper
- 4¼ oz. vegan butter

For serving:

- ½ cup mixed salad greens
- 1 cup vegan mayonnaise
- Juice of ½ a lemon

Directions:

1. In a bowl, mix the flax seed powder with water and set aside to soak for 5 minutes. Then, in a bowl, combine the soy sauce, olive oil, grated ginger, lime juice, salt, and cayenne pepper.
2. Brush the tempeh slices with the mixture. Warm-up a grill pan on medium then grill your tempeh.
3. Remove the slices into a plate and set aside in a warm oven. Grate the broccoli coarsely into a bowl and grate the tofu halloumi cheese on top.
4. Add the flax egg, almond flour, onion powder, salt, and black pepper. Mix the fixings using your hands then create 12 patties out of the mixture.
5. Dissolve the vegan butter in your skillet on medium heat then fry the patties on all sides. Remove the fritters onto a plate.
6. Plate the grilled tempeh with the broccoli fritters, and salad greens. Then, mix the vegan mayonnaise with the lemon juice and serve as a dipping sauce with the tempeh plate.

Nutrition:

Calories: 850

Fat: 71g

Carbs: 18g

Protein: 35g

36. Spicy Veggie Steaks with Green Salad

Prep time: 12 minutes

Cooking time: 20 minutes

Serves: 2

Ingredients:

- 1/3 eggplant
- ½ zucchini
- ¼ cup of coconut oil
- juice of ½ a lemon
- 5 oz. vegan cheddar cheese, cut into small cubes
- 10 kalamata olives
- 2 tbsp pecans
- 1 oz. mixed salad greens
- ½ cup vegan mayonnaise
- salt, as needed
- ½ tsp cayenne pepper to taste

Directions:

1. Rinse the eggplant and zucchini, and cut both vegetables into half-inch-thick slices. Put it in your colander then put some salt. Allow sitting for 10 minutes to let out the liquid.
2. Set the oven to broil then prepare a baking sheet using parchment paper. After 10 minutes, pat the vegetable slices dry with a paper towel and arrange on the baking sheet.
3. Brush with coconut oil and sprinkle with cayenne pepper. Broil until golden brown on both sides, about 15 to 20 minutes.

4. Remove the grilled veggies into a plate then the lemon juice. Arrange the vegan cheddar cheese, Kalamata olives, pecans, plus mixed greens by the grilled veggies. Top with vegan mayonnaise and serve.

Nutrition:

Calories: 512g

Fat: 31g

Carbs: 16g

Protein: 22g

37. Curried Tofu with Buttery Cabbage

Prep time: 35 minutes

Cooking time: 20 minutes

Serves: 4

Ingredients:

- 2 cups water-packed extra firm tofu
- 1 tbsp + 3 ½ tbsp coconut oil
- ½ cup unsweetened shredded coconut
- 1 tsp yellow curry powder
- ½ tsp onion powder
- 2 cups Napa cabbage
- 4 oz. vegan butter
- Salt, as needed
- ground black pepper, as needed
- Lemon wedges for serving

Directions:

1. Place the tofu in between two paper towels to drain liquid for 30 minutes. After, cut into bite-size cubes and drizzle 1 tablespoon of coconut oil on the tofu.
2. In a bowl, mix the shredded coconut, yellow curry powder, salt, and onion powder. Then, toss the tofu cubes in the spice mixture.
3. Warm-up the rest of the coconut oil in a non-stick skillet and fry the coated tofu until golden brown on all sides. Transfer to a plate to keep warm.

4. In another skillet, melt half of the vegan butter, add, and sauté the cabbage until slightly caramelized. Then, season with salt and black pepper.
5. Dish the cabbage into serving plates with the tofu and lemon wedges. Melt the remaining vegan butter in the skillet and drizzle over the cabbage and tofu. Serve immediately.

Nutrition:

Calories: 733

Fat: 61g

Carbs: 8g

Protein: 36g

38. Low-Carb Indian Pasta

Prep time: 5 minutes

Cooking time: 5 minutes

Serves: 4

Ingredients:

- 400 g shirataki pasta
- 2 Roma tomatoes, diced
- ¼ cup diced yellow onions
- ¼ cup green peas
- 1 carrot, diced
- ¼ cup sliced black olives

Vinaigrette:

- 1/4 cup olive oil
- 2 cloves garlic, grated
- ½ tsp red chili flakes
- 1 tbsp lemon juice
- 1 tsp garam masala
- 2 tsp cumin powder
- 1 tsp salt
- ¼ tsp black pepper

Directions:

1. Whisk all the fixings for the vinaigrette in a large mixing bowl. Set aside. Boil your pot filled with water. Blanch shirataki for 1-2 minutes. Drain.
2. Steam carrots and peas. Toss the shirataki, carrots, peas, olives, onions, and tomatoes with the vinaigrette.

Nutrition:

Calories: 157

Fat: 14 g

Protein: 1 g

Carbs: 6 g

39. Vegan Temaki Wraps

Prep time: 10 minutes

Cooking time: 5 minutes

Serves: 4

Ingredients:

- 1 carrot, strips slices
- 1 cucumber, strips slices
- 2 red bell peppers, strips slices
- 200 g button mushrooms, sliced
- 1 1/2 cups uncooked brown rice
- 2 tbsp sesame seeds
- pinch of salt
- 2 sheets nori, cut into squares

Dipping Sauce:

- 1 tsp gochujang
- 2 tbsp sesame oil
- 1 tbsp lime juice
- 2 tbsp low-sodium soy sauce
- 1 tsp erythritol

Directions:

1. Whisk all the fixings for the dressing in a bowl. Warm-up oil in your pan, then cook the mushrooms, flavoring it lightly using salt.
2. When mushrooms are soft, toss in cucumber and peppers. Remove heat then put in the sesame seeds. Wrap in sheets of nori and serve with dipping sauce on the side.

Nutrition:

Calories: 125

Fat: 10 g

Protein: 4 g

Carbs: 8 g

40. Quorn Mince Keema

Prep time: 4 minutes

Cooking time: 20 minutes

Serves: 4

Ingredients:

- 250 g Quorn mince
- 1/4 cup frozen peas
- 2 tomatoes, diced
- 4 cloves garlic, minced
- 1 tsp minced ginger
- 1 shallot, minced
- 2 pcs green chili, deseeded and chopped
- 2 tbsp ghee
- 2 tbsp tomato paste
- 1 tbsp garam masala
- ½ cup coconut milk
- ½ cup water

Directions:

1. Heat ghee in a pan. Add garlic, ginger, and green chili. Sautee until aromatic. Add shallots and tomatoes. Sautee until soft.
2. Add tomato paste and garam masala. Roast briefly. Stir in corn mince. Add coconut milk and water. Simmer within 15 minutes.
3. Put the frozen peas then simmer again within 3 minutes. Flavor it with salt plus pepper if desired. Serve.

Nutrition:

Calories: 125

Fat: 13 g

Protein: 12 g

Carbs: 9 g

41. Gluten-Free Puttanesca

Prep time: 5 minutes

Cooking time: 5 minutes

Serves: 2

Ingredients:

- 2 medium-sized zucchini
- 2 tbsp olive oil
- 4 cloves garlic, minced
- 1 tsp red chili flakes

- 1 shallot, minced
- 1 can diced tomatoes, drained
- 2 tbsp capers
- 10 pieces black olives, sliced
- salt and pepper, to taste

Directions:

1. Process the zucchini in a vegetable spiralizer. Set aside. Warm-up olive oil in your pan. Put the shallots, garlic, plus chili flakes. Sautee until aromatic.
2. Add diced tomatoes, capers, and black olives. Simmer, then flavor it with salt plus pepper. Turn off the heat and toss in spiralized zucchini.

Nutrition:

Calories: 181

Fat: 16 g

Protein: 2 g

Carbs: 9 g

42. Vegan Ma Po Tofu

Prep time: 5 minutes

Cooking time: 5 minutes

Serves: 6

Ingredients:

- 30 g black beans, fermented, chopped roughly
- 25 g peanuts, roughly chopped
- 1 block silken tofu, cut into inch cubes
- 150 g shiitake mushrooms, sliced
- 30 g green onion, thinly sliced

- 1 teaspoon cornstarch
- 1 tablespoon honey
- ½ cup vegetable broth
- 2 tablespoon chili bean paste
- 2 cloves garlic, diced
- 1 teaspoon ginger, diced
- 1 teaspoon Sichuan peppercorns
- 2 teaspoon soy sauce, low sodium
- 2 tablespoon peanut oil
- 1 teaspoon sesame oil
- 1 teaspoon chili oil

Directions:

1. Process the zucchini in a vegetable spiralizer, then put aside. Warm-up olive oil in your pan. Put the shallots, garlic, and chili flakes. Sautee until aromatic.
2. Add diced tomatoes, capers, and black olives. Simmer, flavor it with salt plus pepper. Turn off the heat and toss in spiralized zucchini. Serve.

Nutrition:

Calories: 170

Protein: 7 g

Fat: 12 g

Carbs: 9 g

43. Spicy Carrots and Olives

Prep time: 10 minutes

Cooking time: 10 minutes

Serves: 4

Ingredients:

- ½ teaspoon hot paprika
- 1 red chili pepper, minced
- ¼ teaspoon ground cumin
- ¼ teaspoon dried oregano
- ¼ teaspoon dried basil
- ½ teaspoon salt
- 1 tablespoon olive oil
- 1 pound baby carrots, peeled
- 1 cup kalamata olives, pitted and halved
- juice of 1 lime

Directions:

1. Warm-up your pan using the oil on medium heat. Put the olives, carrots plus the other fixing, toss, cook within 10 minutes, then serve.

Nutrition:

Calories 141

Fat 5.8g

Carbs 7.5g

Protein 9.6g

44. Tamarind Avocado Bowls

Prep time: 10 minutes

Cooking time: 0 minutes

Serves: 2

Ingredients:

- 1 teaspoon cumin seeds
- 1 tablespoon olive oil
- ½ teaspoon gram masala
- 1 teaspoon ground ginger
- 2 avocados, peeled, pitted and roughly cubed
- 1 mango, peeled, and cubed
- 1 cup cherry tomatoes, halved
- ½ teaspoon cayenne pepper
- 1 teaspoon turmeric powder
- 3 tablespoons tamarind paste

Directions:

1. Mix the avocados with the mango and the other ingredients In a bowl, toss and serve.

Nutrition:

Calories 170

Fat 4.5g

Carbs 5g

Protein 6g

45. Avocado and Leeks Mix

Prep time: 10 minutes

Cooking time: 0 minutes

Serves: 4

Ingredients:

- 1 tbsp parsley, diced
- 2 avocados, pitted, sliced
- 2 leeks, sliced
- 1 cup cherry tomatoes, halved
- 1 cup cucumber, slice into cubes
- 1 small red onion, diced

- 1 teaspoon chili powder
- 2 tbsp lime juice
- Salt, as needed
- black pepper, as needed
- 2 tbsp cumin powder

Directions:

1. In a bowl, mix the onion with the avocados, chili powder plus all the fixings, and serve.

Nutrition:

Calories 119

Fat 2g

Carbs 7g

Protein 4g

Conclusion

We hope that we provided you with valuable insight into the Keto vegan way of eating. You will receive nutritional benefits from vegetables, fresh fruits, nuts, beans, whole grains, and soy products. These are some of those benefits and how your health can be affected:

Antioxidants: With this addition, you can protect your body against several types of cancer.

Vitamin C: The C vitamin works as an antioxidant and helps your bruises heal faster and keeps your gums healthy.

Carbohydrates: Your body will tend to burn your muscle tissue if you don't eat plenty of carbs.

Protein: Red meat is not necessarily the healthiest choice for protein. As a vegan, lentils, nuts, peas, beans, and soy products provide this resource without health issues.

Fiber: Vegans experience better bowel movements with increased high fiber in veggies and fruits.

Reduced Saturated Fats: Without meat and dairy products, these levels are lowered immensely.

Magnesium: With the assistance of magnesium, calcium is better absorbed. It is found in dark leafy greens, seeds, and nuts.

Potassium: Acidity and water are balanced by potassium which also leads to a reduction in cancer and cardiovascular diseases.

Here are the tips to achieve success while following a Keto Vegan diet:

- Commit to the 'rainbow' and enjoy a variety of veggies & fruits.

- Include high-fiber starchy options to your diet plan, including brown rice, sweet potato, whole meal bread, whole-wheat pasta, and oats.

- Add plenty of chickpeas, lentils, tofu, and beans

- Be sure to include calcium-rich foods daily, such as calcium-set tofu.

- Be sure to get your omega-3 fats by enjoying seeds and nuts every day.

- Include a variety of herbs and spices instead of table salt.

- Keep your body hydrated, always drink 6 to 8 glasses of liquids daily.

- Start exercising more.

Finally, thank you for your purchase. We hope that you had an excellent time reading. If you felt this book was helpful, let your friends know and share the book with anyone you think might find it useful.

CPSIA information can be obtained
at www.ICGtesting.com
Printed in the USA
BVHW090132240521
607980BV00007B/133